Copyright © 2019 by BARBARA Peters-Howard

All rights reserved. This book or any portion thereof may not be reproduced or used in any manner whatsoever without the express written permission of the publisher. Please send such requests to:
acmpublish@gmail.com

ISBN: 978-1-7329900-4-3

Printed by: A&C Marketplace Publishing LLP in the United States of America

First Printing, 2019

DEDICATION

For all those who like to live in the moment.
Never stop pursuing your destiny,
no matter where you find yourself in life.
Continue moving forward toward the plans
that God has in store for you.

CONTENTS

For His Glory	7
God of Our Fathers	9
Praises	11
Why I Cry	13
What's It All About	15
The Hope Faith	17
Use It or Lose It	19
Knowing	21
Defeat No More	23
The Workplace	25
A Woman After God's Own Heart	27
He Cares	29
The Harvest	31
About the Author	32

FOR HIS GLORY

The Lord is our Shepherd
And we want for no good thing
He is our Bread of Life, our way maker
Jehovah Jireh, our Almighty King
He opens doors that man can't see
Puts order in our lives the way it
Was intended to be
"I knew you before I formed you
In your mother's womb," says the Lord
"You have been chosen by me
Because you are special."
Oh, what a wonderful and mighty God we have
As we offer ourselves unto Him
As a living and holy sacrifice
Leaning on His everlasting arms
Receiving new mercies and grace each day
As we humbly bow in reverence
Giving thanks as we pray
For what God has joined together
Let no man put asunder
So in Jesus name we stake our claim
Sowing seeds, watering, nurturing
Expecting a harvest of prosperity
First from within---without a doubt
Cause our faith will move it inside out
And now our praise is loud and clear
So it will reach our Master's ear
Our arms stretched wide because we have no fear
As His hands reach out to draw us near
Resting under the gracious hand of God
We wipe the dust off our shoes
Leaving the past behind
And pressing forward toward the mark
That we hold so dear within our hearts.

GOD OF OUR FATHERS

We are here to tell the story
Giving almighty God our Father, all the glory
Our Father who is in heaven
Hallowed be His holy name
For He is the God of our destiny
He is the God who sets men free

Yes, our heavenly Father is oh so perfect
And we are still trying to get there
That is why when we open the bible
The written word shows that He cares

For the word tells us that faith and obedience
Are part of the test
Bring your burdens to me and I'll do the rest
Is this the voice you sometimes heard
Sitting quietly not saying a word

Are you called when you are going through
On your worst day you are still called
Continue to labor continue to pray.

PRAISES

We came from a foreign land
From a mighty, mighty long way
We packed our bags
And stored our goods
And sought a brighter day

We couldn't be snobs
Cause we had no jobs
But when we said our grace
It was "Thank you God
For guiding us to another blessed place"

As time went by
Oh, how we did sigh
As we began to shed tears
And sighs of relief
As we continued to watch
An awesome God work wonders of disbelief

He paid our bills
And kept us still
As we panted like deer after water
And now today
Because we obeyed
He has given us brand new quarters.
Amen and Amen

WHY I CRY

I cry because my people hurt
I cry because my people hurt me
I cry because they have buried me alive
That's why I cry

In the church they have hurt me
In their minds I am not set free
In my struggle for survival
I cannot leave things to be
That's why I cry

Life has so many winding roads
And there are many curves in mine
So I seek the Creator of heaven and earth
To beat the odds of time
That's why I cry.

WHAT'S IT ALL ABOUT

What's it all about
What's it all about
It is all about the birth
Of the One who came to earth
The birth of baby Jesus of Nazareth
In the town of Bethlehem

There was Mary – there was Joseph
And the three kings of the Orient
Being led by a star bearing gifts from afar
A star of wonder oh so bright
That was followed throughout the night

Oh! How many knew there was a
Reason for this season
Yet He (Jesus) grew up to be a mighty man
Because the timing was in God's hands

What's it all about
Shall we dance, sing clap hands and shout
Do we really understand
That our Father has made plans
For our Father who is giving
Gives life to the living.

THE HOPE PATH

You think everything is all right
When suddenly there is a slight hold up
What's going on
I know right from wrong
I made a choice
And I used my voice
Saying "Hallelujah! Thank you, Lord"
For we are all on one accord
There is heartfelt hope
Because the chains got broke
We begin again
With a newfound friend
One who sticks closer than a brother
One who is above all others
One who is like no other
And His name is Jesus
He's my friend.

USE IT OR LOSE IT

Which will you choose
No more wasted moments
For I don't want to lose
Those precious gifts that lie within

That need to be pulled out and used
No! No! I don't want to lose
Special gifts just for me
To give new life and set me free
To share with the world
To give joy and hope

These God given gifts
Will we no longer ignore
To father, to mother, to sister, to brother
May the blessings embrace you forever more.

KNOWING

Now I lay me down to sleep
Nor will I cry nor will I weep
With mine eyes I can still see
God's little angels surrounding me

He loves me he loves me not
This is just the enemy's plot
To see you fall and not rise
While he continues to plant more lies

But because the bible tells me so
Our God sits high and sees below
We are His children – trusting in Him
For He is a friend until the end.

DEFEAT NO MORE

There are lights from the streets
There is a lamp under my feet
With the Word as my sword
I see defeat no more.

THE WORKPLACE

Confusion and turmoil
Chaos in the air
Makes you sometimes wonder
If anyone cares

But there's a man upstairs
Who works with toils and snares
He keeps His lines open
For words that have yet to be spoken

He says, "Be still my child
And come draw near
I'm sending you a Comforter
So have no fear"

So it's patience we practice
And faith that we need
In knowing our Creator
Has once again taken the lead.

A WOMAN AFTER GOD'S OWN HEART

Prayer, prayer, prayer changes things
It is like angels taking on wings
For becoming a woman after God's own heart
We must begin with a running start

Through our praise and our worship
And reading of the Word
We'll shout to the heavens
Resting assured, voices will be heard

We stand tall
We walk in faith
We walk boldly
With a steady gait
And as we carry
We do not tarry
To bring His presence in our world.

We learn to lean
So our God can clean
His precious jewels
Outside and in between

He gives us peace and joy everyday
For the power of the cloud of witnesses
Are here to stay!

HE CARES

When you walk with Jesus
All your cares and woes
Will turn to little grains of sand
Because He told you so.

He will build a fence around you
And keep all the links in the chain
For it is He who controls the universe
The sunshine and the rain.

THE HARVEST

I started a little business one day
I wanted to see it grow
But there were just so many little things
I surely did not know

So I sat and I pondered
I thought and I wondered
What makes a garden grow?

Seeds that have been planted
Seeds that have been watered
Prayers that have been chanted
In a season that was quartered

So the seeds that were planted
Was done with lots of love
So now our Father has granted
Sunshine and rain from above

It's harvest time!

ABOUT THE AUTHOR

Ms. Peters-Howard lives in Washington, D.C., and is a native Washingtonian. She graduated from the District of Columbia Public School system. After graduation she studied Accounting at Southeastern University and the former D.C. Teachers College.

Ms. Peters-Howard is a retired Federal Government employee. She is also married and the mother of two children. She is a devout Christian who serves as a Deaconess and member of the Finance Committee at her church.

Using poetry as a form of expressing her love for God. Bringing joy, peace and hope, along with a sometimes quirky view of the Christian life to her readers.